SPIRITUAL DIARY

4-Week

THE PARTHENOS PRESS

Prayer of Repentance

My Lord, God and Savior Jesus Christ, treasure of mercy and spring of salvation, I come to You confessing my sins. I confess that with boldness I dared to defile Your holy sanctuary with my sins. Now I seek Your mercy and love, for Your mercies are boundless: You never turn back a sinner who comes to You. I confess that my mind is burdened with sin and that I have no strength left. Do not turn away from me; do not rebuke me in Your anger nor chasten me in Your displeasure. I am worn out; have compassion upon me, O Lord. Do not judge me according to Your justice, but according to Your mercy. Remember Your creation; do not put me on trial because none of Your servants can justify their deeds. Dress me in a new attire that befits Your glory. Forgive my sins and I shall sing, "Blessed is he whose sins are forgiven." When I confess my sins and reveal my iniquities, you cleanse me. Amen.

Prayer Before Confession

O Holy Father, who desires the repentance of sinners, promising to accept them back; look now, O Lord, at my sinful soul for I have erred and lost my way in the valleys of transgressions for many years, and I am embittered and

PRAYERS

wretched for being removed from the fountain of my salvation. Yet now I come to You, asking to be cleansed from all defilement and filth. Do not reject but accept me. Look at me with compassion and deal with me mercifully and I will be cleansed and saved; do not neglect me lest I perish. Grant me grace that I may approach You with faith and hope, to confess my trespasses and my sins. Enlighten my heart so that I may realize my sins, my mistakes, and my straying. Grant me determination to forsake evil that I may be established in Your commandments and live for the glory of Your holy name. Amen.

Prayer After Confession

I thank Your goodness, O Lover of Mankind because You did not desire that I perish but have awakened me from my slumber and guided me to Your path. You saved me from the valley of destruction and brought me to the safety of Your bosom. Fill me with hope and faith, for I have come to You as the sick one to his physician, an as the hungry to the Spring of living water, as the poor to the Source of riches, as the sinners to the Savior and as the dead to the Fountain of Life; for You are my salvation, my healer, my life, my strength, my comfort my joy, and my rest is in You. Help me, protect me, and teach me to put my will in Your hands, that I may live according to your will. Remove my weakness that I may be firm and continue to be faithful to You until the end. Amen.

Prayer for God's Guidance

Lord, You are aware that I do not know what is good for me, and now that I am about to start (...), how can I know if it is right unless You guide me with Your grace? O Lord, I beseech Your guidance in this matter. Do not let me follow my tendencies if it will cause me to be confused and fall. Keep me from slipping, help me, and let it be according to Your will. If You see it fit, grant me Your blessing to complete it. If not, remove this desire from my heart. You know all things, nothing is concealed from You, Lord I am Your servant, deal with me as You see fit, as I realize that I will have neither success nor peace unless I submit myself to Your will. Teach me to say on every occasion, "Let it be according to Your will, Lord, not according to my own." For Yours is the kingdom, the power, the glory forever and ever. Amen.

Prayer for God's Accompaniment

Grant me Your grace O Lord Jesus, the longsuffering, and be with me that I may dwell in You unto the end. Grant me that I may ask and wish always for what is pleasing to you. Let Your will be my will. Let my will always follow Your will and be in accord with it in a perfect way. Let both of us have one will, for I don't want to desire anything except what You want and what You wish. Grant me not to lust for the things of this world, that I may dwell in You in all things and hold above all things the desire to be as You would have me be and to do as You would have me do. You are the peace of my heart and the shelter of my life. You are the real peace and the only comfort and apart from you everything is hard and confusing. Therefore, in this peace, which is in You, the Great Eternal Good, I am able to rest. For Your I the kingdom and the power and the glory forever. Amen.

✠ Week of ____/____/____ to ____/____/____

Sunday
- ❑ Fasting
- ❑ Other _____

- ❑ 1st Hour (Prime)
- ❑ 3rd Hour (Terce)
- ❑ 6th Hour (Sext)
- ❑ 9th Hour (None)
- ❑ 11th Hour (Vespers)
- ❑ 12th Hour (Compline)
- ❑ Midnight
- # of Prostrations: _____
- ❑ OT:_____
- ❑ NT:_____

Monday
- ❑ Fasting
- ❑ Other _____

- ❑ 1st Hour (Prime)
- ❑ 3rd Hour (Terce)
- ❑ 6th Hour (Sext)
- ❑ 9th Hour (None)
- ❑ 11th Hour (Vespers)
- ❑ 12th Hour (Compline)
- ❑ Midnight
- # of Prostrations: _____
- ❑ OT:_____
- ❑ NT:_____

Tuesday
- ❑ Fasting
- ❑ Other _____

- ❑ 1st Hour (Prime)
- ❑ 3rd Hour (Terce)
- ❑ 6th Hour (Sext)
- ❑ 9th Hour (None)
- ❑ 11th Hour (Vespers)
- ❑ 12th Hour (Compline)
- ❑ Midnight
- # of Prostrations: _____
- ❑ OT:_____
- ❑ NT:_____

Wednesday
- ❑ Fasting
- ❑ Other _____

- ❑ 1st Hour (Prime)
- ❑ 3rd Hour (Terce)
- ❑ 6th Hour (Sext)
- ❑ 9th Hour (None)
- ❑ 11th Hour (Vespers)
- ❑ 12th Hour (Compline)
- ❑ Midnight
- # of Prostrations: _____
- ❑ OT:_____
- ❑ NT:_____

Confession Father Initials: _____

Thursday	❑ Fasting ❑ Other _____
❑ 1st Hour (Prime)	❑ 3rd Hour (Terce)
❑ 6th Hour (Sext)	❑ 9th Hour (None)
❑ 11th Hour (Vespers)	❑ 12th Hour (Compline)
❑ Midnight	# of Prostrations: _____
❑ OT:_____	❑ NT:_____
Friday	❑ Fasting ❑ Other _____
❑ 1st Hour (Prime)	❑ 3rd Hour (Terce)
❑ 6th Hour (Sext)	❑ 9th Hour (None)
❑ 11th Hour (Vespers)	❑ 12th Hour (Compline)
❑ Midnight	# of Prostrations: _____
❑ OT:_____	❑ NT:_____
Saturday	❑ Fasting ❑ Other _____
❑ 1st Hour (Prime)	❑ 3rd Hour (Terce)
❑ 6th Hour (Sext)	❑ 9th Hour (None)
❑ 11th Hour (Vespers)	❑ 12th Hour (Compline)
❑ Midnight	# of Prostrations: _____
❑ OT:_____	❑ NT:_____

Notes

❑ Communion	❑ Tithe
❑ Confession	Book:

Week of ____/____/____ to ____/____/____

Sunday
☐ Fasting
☐ Other _____

☐ 1st Hour (Prime)   ☐ 3rd Hour (Terce)
☐ 6th Hour (Sext)   ☐ 9th Hour (None)
☐ 11th Hour (Vespers)   ☐ 12th Hour (Compline)
☐ Midnight   # of Prostrations: _____
☐ OT: _____   ☐ NT: _____

Monday
☐ Fasting
☐ Other _____

☐ 1st Hour (Prime)   ☐ 3rd Hour (Terce)
☐ 6th Hour (Sext)   ☐ 9th Hour (None)
☐ 11th Hour (Vespers)   ☐ 12th Hour (Compline)
☐ Midnight   # of Prostrations: _____
☐ OT: _____   ☐ NT: _____

Tuesday
☐ Fasting
☐ Other _____

☐ 1st Hour (Prime)   ☐ 3rd Hour (Terce)
☐ 6th Hour (Sext)   ☐ 9th Hour (None)
☐ 11th Hour (Vespers)   ☐ 12th Hour (Compline)
☐ Midnight   # of Prostrations: _____
☐ OT: _____   ☐ NT: _____

Wednesday
☐ Fasting
☐ Other _____

☐ 1st Hour (Prime)   ☐ 3rd Hour (Terce)
☐ 6th Hour (Sext)   ☐ 9th Hour (None)
☐ 11th Hour (Vespers)   ☐ 12th Hour (Compline)
☐ Midnight   # of Prostrations: _____
☐ OT: _____   ☐ NT: _____

Confession Father Initials: _____

Thursday	❑ Fasting ❑ Other _____
❑ 1st Hour (Prime)	❑ 3rd Hour (Terce)
❑ 6th Hour (Sext)	❑ 9th Hour (None)
❑ 11th Hour (Vespers)	❑ 12th Hour (Compline)
❑ Midnight	# of Prostrations: _____
❑ OT: _____	❑ NT: _____
Friday	❑ Fasting ❑ Other _____
❑ 1st Hour (Prime)	❑ 3rd Hour (Terce)
❑ 6th Hour (Sext)	❑ 9th Hour (None)
❑ 11th Hour (Vespers)	❑ 12th Hour (Compline)
❑ Midnight	# of Prostrations: _____
❑ OT: _____	❑ NT: _____
Saturday	❑ Fasting ❑ Other _____
❑ 1st Hour (Prime)	❑ 3rd Hour (Terce)
❑ 6th Hour (Sext)	❑ 9th Hour (None)
❑ 11th Hour (Vespers)	❑ 12th Hour (Compline)
❑ Midnight	# of Prostrations: _____
❑ OT: _____	❑ NT: _____
Notes	
❑ Communion ❑ Confession	❑ Tithe Book:

Week of ___/___/___ to ___/___/___

Sunday	
☐ 1st Hour (Prime)	☐ Fasting ☐ Other _____
	☐ 3rd Hour (Terce)
☐ 6th Hour (Sext)	☐ 9th Hour (None)
☐ 11th Hour (Vespers)	☐ 12th Hour (Compline)
☐ Midnight	# of Prostrations: _____
☐ OT: _____	☐ NT: _____

Monday	
	☐ Fasting ☐ Other _____
☐ 1st Hour (Prime)	☐ 3rd Hour (Terce)
☐ 6th Hour (Sext)	☐ 9th Hour (None)
☐ 11th Hour (Vespers)	☐ 12th Hour (Compline)
☐ Midnight	# of Prostrations: _____
☐ OT: _____	☐ NT: _____

Tuesday	
	☐ Fasting ☐ Other _____
☐ 1st Hour (Prime)	☐ 3rd Hour (Terce)
☐ 6th Hour (Sext)	☐ 9th Hour (None)
☐ 11th Hour (Vespers)	☐ 12th Hour (Compline)
☐ Midnight	# of Prostrations: _____
☐ OT: _____	☐ NT: _____

Wednesday	
	☐ Fasting ☐ Other _____
☐ 1st Hour (Prime)	☐ 3rd Hour (Terce)
☐ 6th Hour (Sext)	☐ 9th Hour (None)
☐ 11th Hour (Vespers)	☐ 12th Hour (Compline)
☐ Midnight	# of Prostrations: _____
☐ OT: _____	☐ NT: _____

Confession Father Initials: _____

Thursday	❏ Fasting
	❏ Other _____
❏ 1st Hour (Prime)	❏ 3rd Hour (Terce)
❏ 6th Hour (Sext)	❏ 9th Hour (None)
❏ 11th Hour (Vespers)	❏ 12th Hour (Compline)
❏ Midnight	# of Prostrations: _____
❏ OT:_____	❏ NT:_____
Friday	❏ Fasting
	❏ Other _____
❏ 1st Hour (Prime)	❏ 3rd Hour (Terce)
❏ 6th Hour (Sext)	❏ 9th Hour (None)
❏ 11th Hour (Vespers)	❏ 12th Hour (Compline)
❏ Midnight	# of Prostrations: _____
❏ OT:_____	❏ NT:_____
Saturday	❏ Fasting
	❏ Other _____
❏ 1st Hour (Prime)	❏ 3rd Hour (Terce)
❏ 6th Hour (Sext)	❏ 9th Hour (None)
❏ 11th Hour (Vespers)	❏ 12th Hour (Compline)
❏ Midnight	# of Prostrations: _____
❏ OT:_____	❏ NT:_____

Notes

| ❏ Communion | ❏ Tithe |
| ❏ Confession | Book: |

Week of ___/___/___ to ___/___/___

Sunday	❑ Fasting ❑ Other _____
❑ 1st Hour (Prime)	❑ 3rd Hour (Terce)
❑ 6th Hour (Sext)	❑ 9th Hour (None)
❑ 11th Hour (Vespers)	❑ 12th Hour (Compline)
❑ Midnight	# of Prostrations: _____
❑ OT:_____	❑ NT:_____
Monday	❑ Fasting ❑ Other _____
❑ 1st Hour (Prime)	❑ 3rd Hour (Terce)
❑ 6th Hour (Sext)	❑ 9th Hour (None)
❑ 11th Hour (Vespers)	❑ 12th Hour (Compline)
❑ Midnight	# of Prostrations: _____
❑ OT:_____	❑ NT:_____
Tuesday	❑ Fasting ❑ Other _____
❑ 1st Hour (Prime)	❑ 3rd Hour (Terce)
❑ 6th Hour (Sext)	❑ 9th Hour (None)
❑ 11th Hour (Vespers)	❑ 12th Hour (Compline)
❑ Midnight	# of Prostrations: _____
❑ OT:_____	❑ NT:_____
Wednesday	❑ Fasting ❑ Other _____
❑ 1st Hour (Prime)	❑ 3rd Hour (Terce)
❑ 6th Hour (Sext)	❑ 9th Hour (None)
❑ 11th Hour (Vespers)	❑ 12th Hour (Compline)
❑ Midnight	# of Prostrations: _____
❑ OT:_____	❑ NT:_____

Confession Father Initials: _____

Thursday
❑ Fasting
❑ Other _____

❑ 1st Hour (Prime)   ❑ 3rd Hour (Terce)

❑ 6th Hour (Sext)   ❑ 9th Hour (None)

❑ 11th Hour (Vespers)   ❑ 12th Hour (Compline)

❑ Midnight   # of Prostrations: _____

❑ OT: _____   ❑ NT: _____

Friday
❑ Fasting
❑ Other _____

❑ 1st Hour (Prime)   ❑ 3rd Hour (Terce)

❑ 6th Hour (Sext)   ❑ 9th Hour (None)

❑ 11th Hour (Vespers)   ❑ 12th Hour (Compline)

❑ Midnight   # of Prostrations: _____

❑ OT: _____   ❑ NT: _____

Saturday
❑ Fasting
❑ Other _____

❑ 1st Hour (Prime)   ❑ 3rd Hour (Terce)

❑ 6th Hour (Sext)   ❑ 9th Hour (None)

❑ 11th Hour (Vespers)   ❑ 12th Hour (Compline)

❑ Midnight   # of Prostrations: _____

❑ OT: _____   ❑ NT: _____

Notes

❑ Communion   ❑ Tithe
❑ Confession   Book:

NOTES

"Seven times a day I praise You, Because of Your righteous judgments."
—Psalm 119:164

"Your word is a lamp to my
feet and a light to my path."
—Psalm 119:105

NOTES

NOTES

"I have heard of You by the hearing
of the ear, But now my eye sees You.
Therefore I abhor myself,
And repent in dust and ashes."
—Job 42:5-6

"Create in me a clean heart, O God, And renew a steadfast spirit within me."
—Psalm 51:10

NOTES

www.ingramcontent.com/pod-product-compliance
Lightning Source LLC
Chambersburg PA
CBHW060609030426
42337CB00019B/3684